In The BLUE SKY

GRAYSCALE COLORING BOOKS

VOLUME 1.

25 | GRAYSCALE PHOTOS

COLOR TEST PAGE

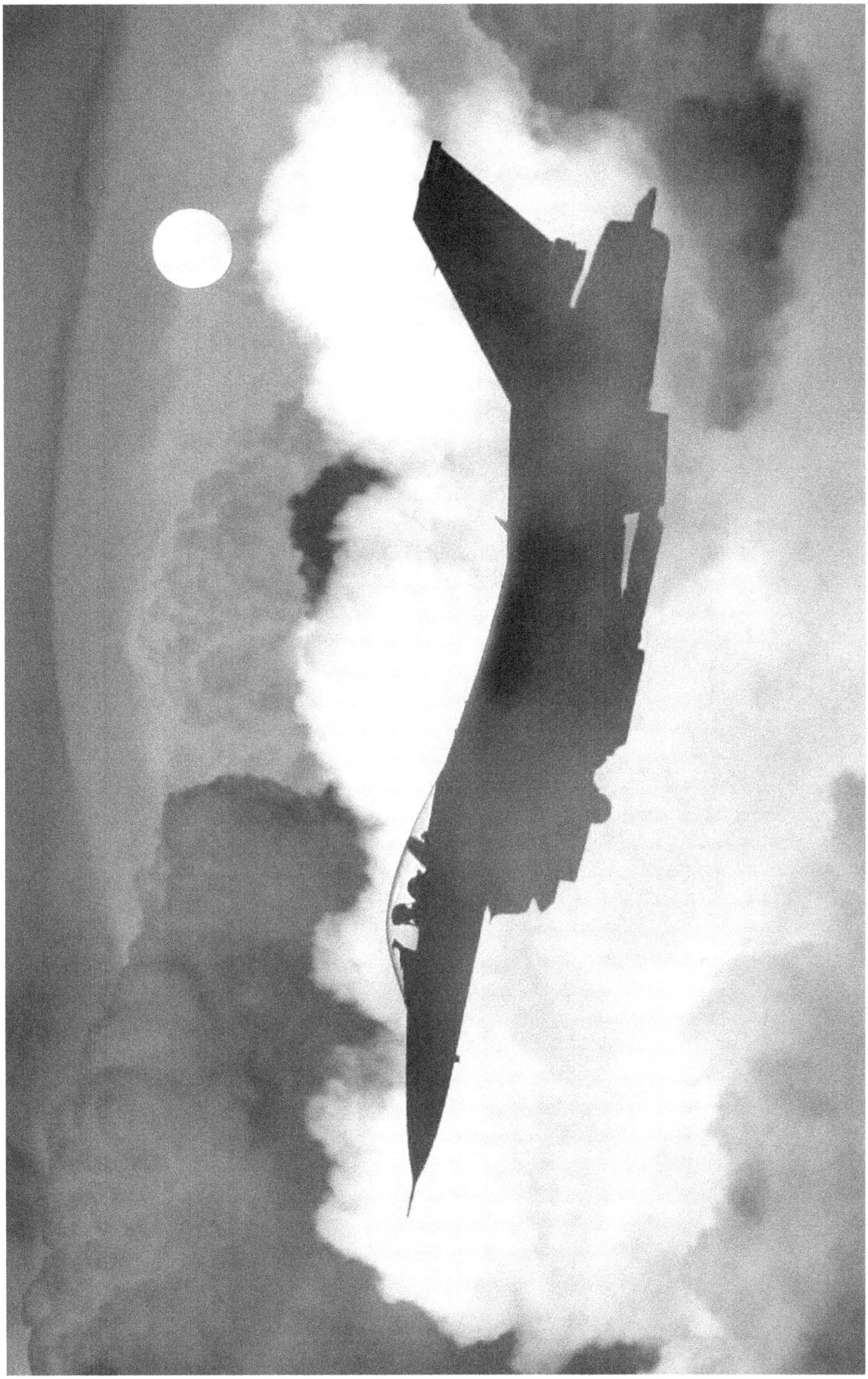

XH558

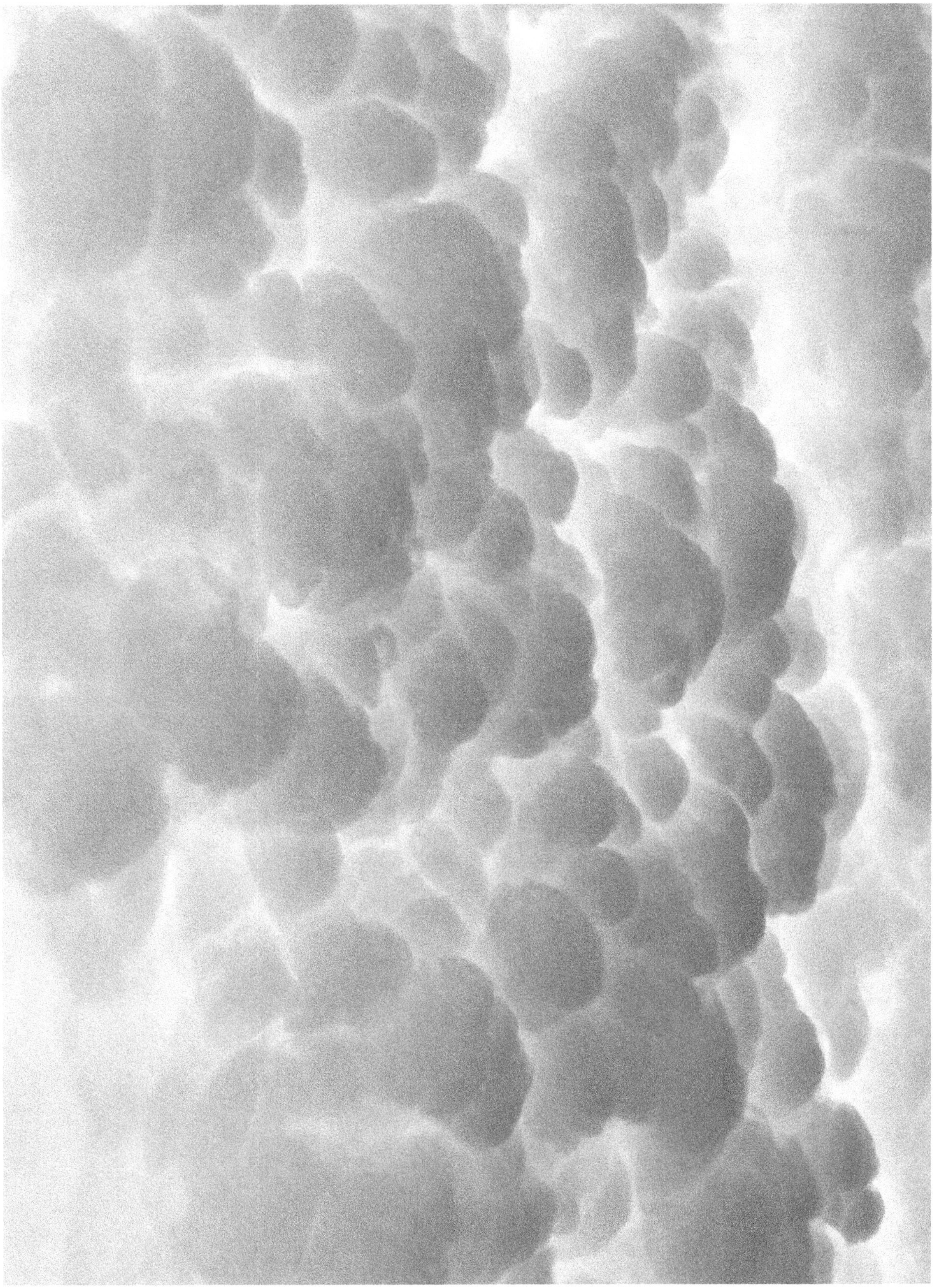

www.ingramcontent.com/pod-product-compliance
Lightning Source LLC
Chambersburg PA
CBHW081120280526
45787CB00007B/2919
9781535136105